PIN UPS

BY
YI SHUN LAI

THE LITTLE BOUND BOOKS ESSAY SERIES
WWW.LITTLEBOUNDBOOKS.COM

LITTLE BOUND BOOKS
WWW.LITTLEBOUNDBOOKS.COM

Published in 2020 by Homebound Publications
Cover & Interior Designed by Leslie M. Browning
Cover Image: by © Jim Holden
ISBN 9781947003897
First Edition Trade Paperback
10 9 8 7 6 5 4 3 2 1

Homebound Publications is committed to ecological stewardship. We greatly value the natural environment and invest in environmental conservation.

For Livia.
May you always know people
who will show you where the trail is.

MY FRIEND ERIK TOOK A SOLO CANOE TRIP down the entirety of the Mississippi River the summer of 2018. He camped at random islands and beaches and parks over three months, and he relied on the kindness of strangers the whole way. This last is one of those plot points that would ordinarily scream cliché if it didn't truly happen, with photos and news coverage to prove it.

This is the kind of trip I'd have fancied myself undertaking at some point; the kind of thing I always knew I could do if I set my mind to it. Such endeavors were the bulk of my aspirations when I was in my teens and early twenties.

Witness the mock cover letter I wrote just after graduating. Aside from listing my accomplishments to date and the reason I wanted to work for so-and-so publication, I also wrote that my biggest goal was to hike the entirety of the Appalachian Trail. My advisers quickly cautioned against including anything of that sort: they said it would look like I was too eager for vacation time.

I'd never thought of it that way. For me, wanting to tackle something like the Appalachian Trail was an indication of dedication, passion, gumption, other things I didn't understand at age 20. Further, it indicated a capability to be At One with the great outdoors and survive on sheer wits and loneliness and sticks of butter, like one hiker I'd read about had done. For a reason I can't pin down, a big outdoors endeavor like this was sexy to me, maybe because of its sheer distance from anything I had ever done before.

It's probably safer to say that thru-hiking the Appalachian Trail was only a symptom of the person I thought I wanted to be: One of those who was at home no matter what the condition. I wanted to be the type to survive out of a little backpack and call it luxurious, say laconically, when people asked me, "What I have is enough," as if "enough" were the most I could ever want.

I'm not sure where I got this idea, because it had certainly never been posited to me in my cushy, advantaged upbringing. And I was never encouraged to get lost in the woods as a child: good girls don't do such things in my culture.

And yet, when Mrs. Salo, my third-grade teacher, read to us from *Wind in the Willows*, I felt a kinship with Mole, lost in the woods and hunting for home with his best friend Ratty. He was immediately a kind of beacon character for me as I, too, looked for something I couldn't find or even define.

Later, in my pre-teens, my mother bought me a subscription to 'Teen magazine. She said it was so I could be more of a girl. She hoped I'd grow out of my loud voice and predilection for jeans and T-shirts, but I skimmed past the articles about makeup and clothes: By then I was already more interested in cutting out the articles about the girls who raced BMX bikes, or the ones who played powder puff football. I remember wanting to surf and ski from the minute I became cognizant these activities existed. I clipped those articles too, and pinned them all to my wall.

I once came close to a version of the life I was pining for: When I was a study-abroad student in

Austria at 16, living with a family in a tiny village in the woods on the Yugoslavian border, my host sister and I spent a good number of evenings bolting through the woods on the bikes, rattling along on forest paths to visit this friend or that in the dappled afternoon light, and then pedaling home long after the sun had gone down by the light of our pedal-powdered lamps. One afternoon, we picnicked by a stream. I leaned against a tree, feeling the first inklings of perhaps belonging somewhere, and ended up with my hair glued to the tree by its sap, which we washed off in the fresh water nearby. Another day, we picked mushrooms, gathering them in baskets. Later, my host mother fried them in butter and herbs and served them atop dandelion greens she'd plucked from her weedy backyard for a dinner salad.

The magazine clippings, the time spent in the woods—they should have made a life, rather than being aspirations and exceptions. I grew up in the foothills of the San Gabriel Mountains, within fifteen minutes of a near-limitless range of trails, one that goes right up to Mt. Baldy, at 10,070 feet elevation. The ocean is a little over an hour away, and I didn't yet have my current irrational fear of sharks.

Mountain biking trails are everywhere, and my 7th-grade Computer Science teacher, Tony Condit, told us he regularly rode his bicycle to Los Angeles International Airport, 51 miles away, for fun.

But when the boys who had moved here to go to college from Oregon and Washington state asked me where to go mountain biking, I couldn't tell them. I can tell them now, but at the time, in a desperate attempt to seem with-it, or, at least, to prove my usefulness, I waved my arm in a manner vaguely northish and said, "Just go straight up the road; you'll end up in the mountains. You can't miss it."

I was already terrified to be seen as not knowing.

I did know where to go skiing, though. I wasn't very good at it, but I fancied myself a regular skier— my parents took us twice a year—and there was one season where I logged in twenty-some odd days on the slopes, playing hooky from Lit 101 and letting that become the thing I was known for in college. I even joined the ski team, run by a guy named Steve who also grew pot plants in the closet of his dorm room.

I was, and still am, a terrible skier. I never could master moguls; I was barely controlled on the black diamonds, and I reverted to the wedge regularly when I panicked. I did get good enough the year of the twenty-something ski days to tackle the steeps, but I wasn't adept enough to warrant my gear, the way I talked about my love of skiing, or even the way I clomped around in my ski boots whenever it got close to ski season, proclaiming that I was just settling into my ski boots, scratching the itch. It wasn't unusual for me to answer my dorm room door in them.

At college I met people who genuinely knew the outdoors, and they supplanted the girls pinned to my wall as new role models. These people, people I actually knew, windsurfed and skied; they'd had knee surgeries by the time they were 18; they rock-climbed and hiked. They did such things as a part of their daily lives!

A few of them took me up Mt. Baldy one time. I wore a pair of mock hiking boots from Marshall's. They had lug treads, though, and if my classmates noticed their thin suede uppers, they were too nice to say anything. We had to come home by a scree field, probably because I was too slow and had set their timing back.

That same year I met my first college boyfriend. He wore a massive knee brace for part of the year because of some surgery or another, could inline skate like no one's business, and kept a rack of CDs of music I'd never heard of in his car. Reggae, if I can recall it, some Blue Öyster Cult, the Moody Blues.

Scott was beyond cool, in my book. He'd road-tripped to college from Oregon with his Honda weighed down by a rack for wind-surfing gear on top of it, and I, trying desperately to keep up, talked up my own sports experience: summer volleyball camp, although I'd never made the team. Track and field, although I only got my varsity letter after two years on JV squad. I had not yet gleaned the difference between these sports, played on groomed fields and slick wooden courts, and the actual outdoors pursuits I was pining for. Surely, I thought, strength and competency in one could substitute for know-how in another.

When you are hungry, you'll eat anything.

I met Scott's friends one summer, when I went to Oregon to be a camp counselor. They invited me to play a game of pickup volleyball with them. I still remember that day: 7 p.m. on a summer evening, the light slanting coyly through old-growth trees; lightning bugs; me, missing spike after spike and set after set and serving into the net with my weak overhand.

Scott and his friends never said a word. It's likely that they were much more gracious than my teenaged brain could have comprehended. I'm sure none of them had ever pretended they knew the words or the melody to a song Scott played on his car's CD deck, for instance, like I did, worrying that if I didn't already know the words he'd brand me a fool as opposed to wanting to introduce me to something he loved. And I'm sure that none of them ever actually needed to hear him reprimand them: "That would be easier if you actually knew the words," he'd said one day to me, gently, nearly under his breath.

When he eventually left for another college more suited to his lifestyle, I took a windsurfing class by way of homage. I was okay at it, but the equipment investment was huge, and I didn't love it.

I puzzle through these goals I had set for myself. I wonder why they seemed so attractive at the time. I wonder why it took me so long to realize that actually being any of those things—a surfer, a BMX biker, an adept outdoorswoman—required much more than tacking photos of women doing those things up on my wall, and half-hearted school team tryouts. I wonder why I didn't understand how far the track, the volleyball court, the field, was from mountains, ocean, lake, trail.

Even now, twenty years after those confused days, when I scroll through the Facebook feeds of friends who always have been and always will be better than I am at such things, there is a distant sense of false nostalgia, a wistful pull to try again for what some friends affectionately call the dirtbag lifestyle.

Ah, I could say it's simple: I like wine and matching pajamas. I like cocktail bars and expensive clothing and museums of almost any sort. I prefer to close a vacation day with a quiet dinner and a pint at a bar over crawling, hunch-backed, into a tent, and having to filter my own water. I hate lighting up those cranky Primus stoves.

I do not love being dirty for too long.

But I love the outdoors with a distracting kind of joy. I can lose hours in the simple contemplation of it. I can stare at a stormy sea day after day and watch the sun sear the desert for those same days. Every day I leave my home to walk my dog I marvel at the same horizon, in markedly different colors. Each time I go outside, something is different, and interesting, worth noticing.

My body is capable, and strong. I keep it that way for reasons well beyond the fact that I also like clothing that looks like it fits bespoke to me. I go to great lengths to stay strong so that I can enjoy the outdoors. I dedicate hours to it, hours to getting outside. Last week, I crashed my bike, and I spent the hours in the ER wondering how long until I could get back on it.

But at some point in my early twenties, I started thinking this lifestyle for me was never going to be a possibility: I had chosen a career that required me to live in New York City. I had gradually lost touch with the friends who could introduce me to that lifestyle. Or, if they were still around, I had cultivated this persona of a woman who already knew those things, and so didn't need introduction or hand-holding to get to know them, and I didn't feel I could let that delusion go, or disabuse my friends of that notion.

*   *   *   *

In Taiwan, where I was born and lived until I was four, they say that if you praise your children too loudly, the gods will overhear, and they will want the child for their own. It's a grim prospect.

But some parents get carried away. In high school, my parents warned me not to hang out with certain girls, because I would most certainly get compared unfavorably just standing next to them. When I went for jogs, trying to lose the weight from a particularly delicious semester in Paris, I was greeted with jeers and mocking rejoinders: "Oh! We were driving down the street and I thought to myself, 'Who's that fat girl? Why, it's my own daughter!' I laughed and laughed."

As often happens with parental units, one was kinder than the other: "I was walking down the street and I saw a young lady walking on her way to work," said my dad. "She was passing a car and leaned down to see her reflection in the window. She checked her lipstick. I thought to myself, 'Maybe one day this will be my daughter, on her way to work, checking what she looks like.'"

I won't get into why I think they did this. I don't think I care anymore, except to poke around back there and figure out what about all that made me who

I am today, and how that plays into what we know of ourselves as human beings, what makes these motivations so critical to forming our adult selves, and how they inform our interactions.

But I also poke around to get to know myself more. It's a very satisfying form of navel-gazing. If you can get at what got you to where you are now, maybe you can finally figure out how to get at what you really want. Or even, what what you want actually is.

*   *   *   *

Maybe I knew early on I'd never be one of the girls my parents admired, and so maybe I was looking for a way to stand out in the ways that no one expected. But getting there would be going into unmarked territory: my parents didn't seem to know anyone who preferred mountains and sea to offices, malls, and restaurants, much less surfers, skiers, people on bicycles. So I had to feel my own way, and it was only until I moved to one of the world's largest metropolises that I discovered outdoors sports, in genuine fashion.

I spent a couple summers in Boston and met a guy who loved bicycles. He was a mechanic at a bike shop, and he'd been roommates with the guy who loved to windsurf. And he showed me his kind of outdoor recreation, which had been largely ingrained in him as a child.

The same parents who had shown Andy how to ski, sail, and hike were also doctors in the heart of Boston, and so he'd grown up with all the cultured things my parents had weaned me on, as well. It was the perfect starter package, for someone who wanted so desperately to be an outdoorsperson in some fashion.

We hiked those summers and I learned to properly ride a bike, and by the time I graduated and was living in New York, I'd signed Andy and me on to ride from Boston to New York, in a charity ride. I met new friends at the training rides, spent money on riding kit, grew to love this thing that introduced me to new places and new people, at speed.

Oh, don't get me wrong. I was still a dedicated gym rat. And I joined a club volleyball team, because apparently I wasn't over beating that drum yet. But that led, eventually, to a group called the Hash House Harriers, where there was a minority of women who ran with a majority of men. The runs always started and ended at a bar, and I was already good at drinking, since I was in my twenties and living in New York City. These people became my pack, and through this pack I met a guy whom I eventually dated and through whom I eventually, and finally, truly learned what it meant to enjoy the outdoors as an athlete.

Which is still weird to people, because who learns about the outdoors living in New York City?

It was there, too, that I met women who not only had had the same aspirations I did, but who had been acting on them—who were doing the things I had wanted to do—all those years.

It's been almost twenty years since then, and I can still trace every outdoors activity I ever participated in to some guy I was dating or had slept with. In other words, I didn't manage to meet women who were actually *playing* in the outdoors until I had worked my way through way too many men.

The whole time I was flailing, I used my temporary aspiration as an outdoors journalist to meet people who did these things: wolf biologists, surfers in New Jersey, folks who were bicycling across the country, fly fishermen. They were nice. But they weren't peers; they were subjects, part of my job.

And there was a moment where part of my job veered dangerously close to a move to Montana, drawn, again, by that shimmering mirage of an outdoor lifestyle, and aided by the fact that I'd known a guy who lived there and slept with him. There, too, I thought maybe I'd take on the cloak of his life when I got there, although I didn't admit that to myself.

I went to Montana. I put down first month's rent on a lease. I rented a moving truck. My best friend at the time blocked out a week to move me, and another friend bought plane tickets to visit me. But I woke up in a cold sweat two nights in a row, and, at 3 a.m. one morning, called Julia to tell her that I didn't think I should move after all.

I know now that if I had gone, I might be one of those people who lives in a place rife with outdoors opportunities and has no idea how to access them. I hope not, but you never know.

*   *   *   *

The guy I dated at the Hash House Harriers introduced me to adventure racing, a sport in which one kayaks, mountain-bikes, orienteers, and sometimes rappels, and whatever else the race director wants.

More importantly, it was there that I met women who also did these things, although they were just the women I drank with at the time. They were elite athletes in their own fashion, accomplished mountain bikers and road cyclists and long-distance runners and triathletes, and they did it locked in with skyscrapers and 10-hour workdays, just like me.

I couldn't really reconcile it in my own head at the time. Manhattan was for running and casual inline skating in the park. New York City was for club sports and dance classes, at the best. I'd resigned myself to three-mile runs and thrice-weekly visits to the gym. The Hash House Harriers pushed me to five, then eight, miles, more if you counted all the getting lost one did on a hash run.

But could a girl also pursue the real outdoors here?

Then I met Jody. Jody matched us, pint for pint, shot for shot, cocktail for cocktail. The first night I met her, my date said, "Oh, that's Jody. She makes the best Jell-o shots." Sure enough, they came in horse syringes.

Jody came to most Girls' Nights Out and was my plus-one at more events than I can remember. But she was always the first to leave, begging off so she could get in enough sleep before her 5 a.m. workout the next day.

And then there was Jen. Jen works like crazy, too. She's an amateur oenophile and salsa-dances with a passion. She'd run a couple marathons by the time I met her, and would go on to run several more.

And Lara. She completed a two-day adventure race in West Virginia in the early stages of her pregnancy. She trained for it while living in Manhattan. I'm not sure she ever even made it to the outer boroughs.

Me? "Long-distance running," for me, was six, seven miles. I could ride a bike forever, sure, but more importantly at that point in my life, I could drink. The girls and I met on that point, at least, and suddenly, something clicked into place.

These women were my role models because they were close enough to touch. They made regular-enough appearances in my line of sight to ingrain sport and the outdoors into my life.

With the women of Girls Night Out humming in the background, I cancelled my gym membership and went outside. I learned to paddle, orienteer, and snowshoe, since adventure racing takes place year-round. I got very good at trail running, and eight-minute miles over rough terrain became a regular benchmark. Eventually I transitioned from road bike to mountain bike, and that's how I met my husband, who is endlessly patient and doesn't mind teaching me new things or working with me to refine things I'd like to learn, and who—alas!—is yet another man in my long, ragged history of sport.

*   *   *   *

I'm utterly fascinated by the field of leadership studies. Point me to a TED Talk about organizational psychology, and look for me hours later, deep in a rabbit warren generated by that one study the speaker referenced and bolstered by whatever studies *that* study may have leaned on for its results. One more hour later, and I'm in the Amazon pages, picking up books written about those studies.

Women in leadership is a particularly deep hole for me to fall into: I'm fascinated by the studies that explore how and why some women treat each other badly in workplaces. Anecdote after anecdote, study after study, I parse how to be a better leader, a more supportive person.

Psychologists have posited everything from a deep biological drive—women have always had to compete for mates, and the workplace is a version of that, they say—to tokenism, the curious situation by which the sole "other" in any group begins to take on the attributes of the majority, just to be able to fit in. (This is where you find the women who claim they're "just one of the guys," or "not like other women.")

But in the world of sport, where things are judged on a much more animal level—faster, stronger, more agile—maybe it isn't as hard to buoy another of your gender, and not as hard to welcome them into your midst.

Whatever the reason, it wasn't until I found the women who adventure-raced, the big dogs in my pack, that I began to settle into the possibility that outdoor sport was even a remote possibility for me. Sure, there was an element of odd-woman-out, still: Most racing teams I knew of comprised three men, one woman; or two men, one woman. Every once in a while you'd see a duo of women making their way across the race course, but you'd usually find mixed-gender couples racing. (The premium division in adventure racing is co-ed, and the sport was conceived as a co-ed endeavor.)

In adventure racing, I felt welcome, and then at home. Whether that was due to the paucity of women I encountered or the more level playing field I couldn't tell you. Or maybe it was because there were so many new things to learn that everyone was hopeless at something: That guy with the runner's legs was probably a terrible navigator. The strong paddler might very well be an awful climber, or afraid of heights. And the person who was good at all of those things was probably just a bad teammate. We knew one guy who was so driven he destroyed his calf forcing himself through a cramp, taking the entire team out of commission.

I'd finally found a place where it was okay to be semi-competent, or not competent at all, so long as you were improving, or you would walk out of a class or an event having learned something new.

In adventure racing, it seemed, no one was expert. Everyone made mistakes, even if they were as basic as leaving your maps in your gear bin, leaving your team with no way of navigating, or falling asleep on your bicycle, or packing the wrong food. You toed the start line with the professionals, the teams who took home cash prizes and who were sponsored, and teams were encouraged to help each other on the race course.

I had finally found a song you didn't need to know all the words to in order to be part of the in-crowd. And even though it was another relationship that had landed me there, I was finally rooting around in mud and exploring the landscape and hanging out with people I liked for long periods of time, over long training days. I never did learn how to ride a BMX bike, but I did get to be pretty good on a bicycle, either road or mountain, and it was in the bike saddle that I finally figured out what it meant to feel adept. And confident.

It's easy now to see why I failed in those early years of finding a home in sport. I didn't look for women. And I certainly didn't look for the women who looked like me, who shared my features, sure, but who also shared my culture, my background.

I didn't understand that they existed.

*   *   *   *

I have spent most of my life swaddled in privilege: My parents paid for my expensive private-college education; they helped me through a rough spot when I first started freelancing, and my husband's steady job affords us great health insurance, as well as a backup salary should I have a lean month or two freelancing. We own two cars and five bicycles between us, and live in a pretentious little suburb of Los Angeles, the kind with a Coffee Bean and Tea Leaf, Starbucks, *and* a Pain Quotidien.

It's embarrassing to realize now that I've gravitated naturally to sports that are equipment-heavy and whose competitions come with hefty entrance fees.

Take skiing, for instance. What is it about all that equipment that appeals to anyone? Big, clunky boots; poles; helmets, goggles, snowsuits taking up valuable closet real estate. I lived in Southern California when I got into skiing, for goodness' sake. You have to make a gargantuan effort to find a need for snowsuits.

Road riding, the type where you get on a bike that can take you from Boston to New York, is no different. You buy an expensive bike (the road bike in my garage now cost me $5,000 in 2008). Then there's all the expensive Lycra and Spandex. And the shoes, which always run upwards of $100, but which, fair play, do last for an awfully long time. Oh. And the helmet, obviously. Gloves, lights. Handlebar-top computer, to tell you precious little things like your cadence and your speed.

Rock climbing's another. Seems so pure, doesn't it? You, the rock, the sunrise. Nope: Grippy shoes, $100. Chalk bag, $30. Harness, $50, minimum. You can wear your own pants and stuff, but ooh, once you get to the fancy rock, you are going to want some ropes and an ATC and some handy carabiners, which, okay, you can also use to hang your handbag off a restaurant table with. Very multi-tasky, those carabiners. But that harness you're only going to wear out for one purpose. Trust me. And how do you think you're going to get to all those legendary rocks? You're not going to do it on the inter-city bus, that's for sure.

Oh, city rock gyms, you say? It's not a mistake that you're apt to find those in the more tony parts of town: The one I used to go to is in New York's Lincoln Square, just down the street from Lincoln Plaza and the Metropolitan Opera. (There's another cheaper one closer to Hell's Kitchen, but it wasn't as convenient as the one in Lincoln Square.)

Adventure racing is the mother of all gear sports, since it's a minimum of three sports rolled up into one event. Your running shoes you will need to be very, very grippy. Dedicated trail runners, at least. Gaiters to go with those, so you won't get too much dirt in your shoes. Then you will want a good, sturdy mountain bike, and another pair of shoes that you can both clip into your bike in and walk in, because the terrain is tricky and not always bike-friendly. Then you will need a paddle, for the canoe or kayak leg, and your own life jacket. You want a good compass. Then you can start thinking about clothing and required equipment: lightweight first aid kit, knife, wicking everything and waterproof everything else. It adds up really, really fast.

At some point in my bicycling and adventure racing life, and probably after I'd become too lazy to pack all of that adventure racing gear every weekend for multi-sport workouts with friends, I became interested in triathlon. And then, a slow, ugly dawn came upon me. All these sports, every single one I have ever invested in, are majority white.

*   *   *   *

Mind you, I'm pretty sure I didn't understand I was anything other than white until my mid-twenties.

Probably something to do with the whole model-minority thing: you know, keep your head down and don't make waves, and it'll be better for everyone involved. Also something to do with the company I kept: mostly upwardly mobile, white professionals.

There were moments when I had it made obvious to me that I wasn't the same, like the day I was mistaken for one of the other rare Asians on a bike course. Picture it, won't you?

Guy: Hey! How'd you get over here so fast?

Me: Sorry?

Guy: You were just over there. *Waves in general, far-away direction*

Me: Mmm. No. I've been here, pretty much, the whole time. Eating.

Guy: No. It was you. But you've...changed.

Me: Wait.

Guy: You were wearing pink before.

Me: I don't own any pink cycling jerseys. That wasn't me. I know who you're thinking of. That was Angela.

Guy: It was you.

Me: She was wearing a pink Western-style cycling jersey. And I don't know where she got it, but some kind of cowboy hat. Right?

Guy: Yeah!

Me: Not me.

Guy: It was you.

This experience so branded me for life that, years later, when a man insisted that he'd met me before and I couldn't dredge up the memory, I impatiently passed a hand over my face and said, "We all look alike, okay?" It turns out, he *had* met me, and I'd just been too annoyed at his insistence to really think about it.

Other Asian Girl and I wrote to each other for a little while. I wish I'd hung onto her address. I tell you what, even if you think you're actually white, deep down inside, you know you're different, and that gets lonely, fast, and it was nice to know there was someone else out there (shit, where did she live, even? Ohio? New Jersey?), pursuing the same things, someone who understood.

Angela? Is that even right?

Dammit.

*   *   *   *

You know, I used to think it was good to stand out. But now I know better. You get tired of being the girl who's "so articulate." Or "so outgoing." Or "so loud." Or "so outdoorsy." Because all of that stuff, if you're me, living here in America, comes with the unspoken addendum: "...for an Asian girl."

Some days, the addendum is spoken, like the day an older gentleman approached me after a writing workshop expressly to inform me that he thought I had adjusted *so* well to life in the United States. That he'd have thought I was American if I wasn't Asian.

And maybe that's why, all those years ago, I had all those things tacked up on my wall, why I hunted down all those stories and people to report on and emulate, why I developed this persona in the first place: I'm searching for what it means to be me, and I'm not happy with the idea that the things I love to do and the interests I take necessarily mean I have to be the "loud Asian girl," or "the outspoken Asian girl." Or even just "unusual."

*   *   *   *

Not long ago, my husband and I took my parents up to Carmel-by-the-Sea, a coastal California town, for the annual Bach festival there. It was so bougie, if you'll excuse the expression: lots of people decked out in their West-Coast dress-up; all slacks and suit jackets; wine and beer sponsors; an extensive spread of crudités and flatbreads before each show. There was an arts auction.

We're in our forties, my husband and I, and it is very much time for us to think about our retirement plans. Over the years, we've gradually honed in on some basic requirements: We want a natural water feature, either the ocean or some mountain lakes. I finally figured out that I didn't want a tourist community; I wanted a year-round community, and a good local bookstore would be the best indicator of that. Add that to the requirements list.

And finally, we want to feel safe. Correct that: *I* want to feel safe. My husband, a balding, middle-aged white guy, can feel safe anywhere.

In Carmel, the median income is $87,532. Every other car in downtown seems to be a Merc or a Lexus or some other type of foreign luxury car. The town was founded by Irish immigrants, so there are faux thatched roofs or actual thatched roofs everywhere, and a great many of the boutiques are so precious you want to squee, like how you can't drive past a bunch of cows without going, "Moo." The town library, right on the main street, is robust, stocked full of great books. People are friendly; the retail and service industries are thriving, and my parents have friends there. Hell, I ran into someone I know there. Over the weekend, we went for jogs and looked at the ocean and walked a lot and ate well.

The population is majority white, but there's a healthy minority population, too: 3.3% Asian; 13.3% Hispanic; 3% mixed-race. Way lower percentages than I'd like to see for Blacks and Native Americans, but you take what you can get, I guess.

Sometime during our weekend, an unwelcome realization began creeping up on me: Here, in this wealthy, marginally diverse enclave of not-quite-real-life, I felt relaxed.

Safe.

In major American cities, I also feel safe, and relaxed. But that's not the place we want to retire to.

The corollary to that creeping knowledge is the one no daughter who's tried to make a name for herself wants to confront, ever: My parents were right. It is better, it feels better, when one can be among one's own people, even if you have to define "one's own people" by where they sit in the economic strata.

For someone who's tried to buck the system, who's wanted to see herself as being able to surmount the disadvantages of wearing her minority on her face; for someone who's wished, so many times over, to just be able to fit in someplace, find her own tribe, well, this is like finally waving the (literally) white flag.

I give up. I can only be comfortable among my own kind, with people who go to the same kinds of events I do and who value the same kinds of values I do, who drive the same kinds of cars. They might be white, and I might be Asian, but there is a reason Asian Americans are called the "model" minority: Who do you think we're modeling ourselves after?

Well, ain't that a kick in the pants.

*   *   *   *

In tokenism, the first to do anything—the first Black man, say, to break into the Rat Pack, á la Sammy Davis Jr., or the first woman to break the CEO ranks, á la Anna Bissell or Katharine Graham—often does so at the expense of the values that come connected to their own identities. Sammy Davis Jr. was shunned by Black Americans for his friendship with Richard

Nixon. Anna Bissell is remembered by history as being "aggressive"; Graham was famously slow coming to the feminist movement. In my case, I eschewed everything my parents thought I should be. I was terrible at science and math in school, although I'm deeply curious about animal biology and ecology. I don't think I was ever the obedient, quiet Asian girl: stories of my frog voice calling for my cousins across abnormally long distances from the time I could speak are family legend.

I didn't rebel in "classic" ways, like getting into hard or prescription drugs, and I wasn't especially promiscuous, although when I finally left the quiet California town after college for New York, I had a longish, healthy relationship with a series of one-night stands. For a long time, I traded on brashness, on volume, on pretending I knew more than I actually did. I wanted to make it despite myself.

I haven't figured out a way to do this yet.

It's okay to be a token in some areas of life. Work, for instance, because representation matters, and if you're not showing people you can break the glass ceiling, or that you can hold just as high a position or be just as aggressive as the next guy, then nothing will ever get better for anyone. And in some cases, like in my own grapple with where I belong in the world of outdoor sport, it's probably less about tokenism and more about demonstrating the presence of a gender or an ethnicity in sport.

This is, potentially, why sport is so attractive to me. If you are successful in sport, it's likely not because you're a token—it's because you're just good at what you do. The literal playing field is more likely to be even.

There are some areas in which it's just physically unsafe to be a token or a pioneer. In 2008, during one of my very last adventure races ever, my friend Hans, a tall, Germanic guy on a team with a tall, Germanic girl and Hans' ginger friend Chris, got plastic bottles thrown at him as they were riding down the street in a rural community.

If Hans can get attacked just for doing something that looks out of the ordinary, then what hope do I have for doing anything out of the ordinary?

I don't mind being called a bitch, or being told to shut my big mouth. What I know I'd really mind is some version of what happened in another race, where we were in a convenience store picking up some soda (you can do this during an adventure race, which is one of the reasons I love them), and I got into line behind a little girl and her dad. Her dad smiled at me, I smiled at the little girl, and then she very slowly, and deliberately, put her fingers to the corners of her eyes and pulled them upwards.

Her father's smile turned apologetic, and so I let it go.

It's more likely that I read it as an apologetic smile, because I was in rural Illinois at the time, and didn't want to kick up a fuss. Plus, if I had said something to her father, or maybe directly to her, like "That wasn't very nice," I don't think I could stand the heartbreak if he then chose to fling some kind of racial slur at me. That would have been too much.

I'd like to paddle, like my friend Erik, down the Mississippi, through the undiscovered regions of this wonderful nation I call home. But the stakes feel too high for me. I can put my body at risk doing the things I love—mountain biking, rock climbing, snowshoeing. But these dangers are my choice. What tips the scale; moves the needle, is having that choice taken away from me.

What makes not getting to do an Erik canoe trip so heartbreaking is that, paddling through

Minnesota, Iowa, Illinois, Wisconsin, Missouri, Tennessee, Arkansas, Mississippi, Louisiana, I'd want to dawdle with the wildlife, float in a couple of places, camp on whatever spit of beach I see. I'd want to talk to the locals, sample the local foods, read the local paper, get to know each little town on the river.

In some of these places, I'm not sure the towns would want to get to know me. In some of these places, I wouldn't be welcome. And while I have had good experiences in little towns, I've also had plenty of bad experiences, where the room chills, perceptibly, or goes quiet when I and my parents walk in, or where you just get stared at a little. Too. Long.

*   *   *   *

Women do hike alone, canoe alone, travel alone. I have a good number of female acquaintances who travel alone all the time. They are typically white, but Rahawa Haile, an Eritrean-American, actually fulfilled my own short-lived pipe dream of hiking the Appalachian Trail, and she wrote extensively about her experience, mentioning other Black thru-hikers. I read her powerful article hoping to find some way out of my cocoon of fear, but her experience was largely what I thought it'd be, fear and loneliness and contemplation, although she does end on an upnote about the community she found on-trail. (By the way, it's worth noting that when I looked up "Black hikers Appalachian Trail" to read more about her experience, Google spat out an advertising result for a black Salomon trail running shoe. It's model number XA Pro 3D, and it's $116.95.)

In the woods now, I see Asian women mountain biking, and here in Southern California, it's not unusual to run into great strings of Asians, Koreans, and Japanese and once, even, a tiny group of Taiwanese visitors, hiking Mt. Baldy. We had a chat in our native language, bantering about the mountain and my relative youth and inappropriate tiredness. My heart hiccupped a little, experiencing this little slice of home so far from Taiwan itself.

And in the early 1900s, the golden age of exploration, although men went to Antarctica, Papua New Guinea, and the North Pole, women went on adventures, too. Edna Brush Perkins and a friend put on some pants (scandal!) and drove across the Mojave Desert in a wagon in the 1920s. In 1871, Lucy Walker summited the Matterhorn and the Eiger, becoming the first woman to do so. And yet, in history, we only hear about the men. Women were largely expected to stay out of the public eye, and so they didn't do things like seeking honor or prestige or funding from the public. They didn't go on great lecture tours, espousing their work.

And if they wrote books, like Brush Perkins did about her adventure in the Mojave and then her adventure in the Sahara, sweeping, tender books with funny conversational asides that make you feel like you were exploring with these women; books that still manage to capture the very nature of these places they visited, these books were pooh-poohed by the literary editors of publications like *The London Standard* as being "attractive—if somewhat 'thin,'" and the writer deemed "not ... equal to an adequate description" of the places they had been.

Which is interesting, because this is the 1920s, and London is a long way away from Death Valley, and I am damn sure that reviewer had never set foot in the Mojave himself.

In the most comprehensive note I've yet to find about Edna Brush Perkins, her work in charity and social reform is listed, along with details of her family. It says she was a "poet, published travel writer, and pianist." Never mind that she was a gutsy, ballsy explorer. Never mind *that*.

There is a good amount written about the 17th-century Dutch illustrator Maria Sibylla Merian, who was one of the first to conduct an independent visit to Suriname in order to study the flora and fauna there. Her work shows the lifecycle of insects, from egg to pupae to death, but she also was one of only illustrators of the time to draw the creatures in situ, without killing them and mounting them on pegs. I learned this from a docent at the National Museum of Women in the Arts.

My friend Kate has been working on a series for Outside Magazine Online where she finds and writes about overlooked women in sport. It was through her post that I learned about Lucy Walker.

And recently, my friend Mike posted on Facebook about his daughters' visit to the Singapore Grand Prix. The post is accompanied by a photo: in it, his two daughters, aged eight and 10, are taking a selfie next to a gorgeous woman in full makeup wearing a racing suit. "Girls were psyched to meet a female driver," reads Mike's post.

That post was the first thing on my screen this morning when I woke up my computer. I suppose it's an indication of how saturated my feed is now with stories of fantastic women, that a piece of media that lifts me so can be the first thing I see, by chance.

And actually, the effect of seeing these posts is the same as seeing those articles tacked onto my wall when I woke up every morning as a pre-teen. The difference is the medium, of course, but Edna Brush Perkins and that damn review of her book also have a permanent place on the bulletin board in my office, as a reminder that women have gone before. And that, if they didn't experience tokenism, it's because they were never even given a chance to.

*   *   *   *

I'm reminded of a particular evening in New York City. I was on my way to meet a friend after a long day's work. I popped out of the subway station at Central Park South and 57th, added a little forward lean to my gait to compensate for the wind whipping around the buildings. I rounded the Time-Life building, squeezing between a Halal Kebab cart and the wall, and spotted the shadow of a woman, looking brisk and efficient, collar popped against the wind, making her way around the corner.

"Hm," I thought to myself, echoes of my father's sentiment creeping through my brain, "that's the kind of woman I want to grow up to be."

It was a split second before I realized that the shadow belonged to me.

When I'm on my bike, I often check my shadow, to ensure steady shoulders and an even cadence; to look for a straight back and good posture. Here in sunny southern California, there aren't many days when I don't see my shadow.

In shadow form, I'm not any particular ethnicity. I'm just a woman.

Perhaps it's enough, this. To be just a woman, not an ethnicity or a minority, with all of that ensuing baggage.

In fact, it might even be preferable.

*   *   *   *

The women in my life are extraordinary creatures. They populate my daily Facebook feed with pictures of themselves among mountains and big, big trees.

One of them guides blind athletes through things like very long triathlons, and week-long cross-continental bicycle races. Another is a former Olympic mountain biker. Some are adventure racers; one is a champion stand-up paddler; another is an ultra-marathoner who loves mountains. Another does CrossFit, still another used to run a Barre studio; still another does martial arts like nobody's business. A good number of these women are minorities. Asians, even.

If I pay close attention to the way I feel when I look at their posts and how they affect me, I get a distant sense of community. I don't belong to these women's social circles, exactly, and I don't indulge in the same sports they do.

What I get is a weird sense of broadening. Of expanse and possibility.

And, most comfortingly, of normalcy.

*   *   *   *

Vanessa Hua, an Asian-American writer whose book of short stories was published around the same time as my novel, published again in late 2018. This time, her novel was published by Penguin Random House, one of the biggest publishing houses in history, and Vanessa has had great success on lots of different levels: national appearances, reviews, and so on.

In a blog post at a highly visible, highly regarded literary magazine, Vanessa used the space allotted her to discuss, briefly, the stereotype of the Asian immigrant. And then, she used the rest of the space to discuss each of the books and authors that has come with her on this journey of subverting the stereotype. The list of authors she names is long. Mine is among them, and this act of Vanessa's has evoked the same sense that I get from seeing the posts of the women I admire doing the things they love: Together we form a kind of loose community. I see you, says this community. I have gone before, and you can come with me, the next time I do this thing. You are welcome here.

*   *   *   *

I did eventually go on to do an Ironman triathlon, even though I'd said many times I had no desire to do such a thing. As I got to know more triathletes outside of Jody, it just became a thing that I should maybe try.

And so it crept up on me, sprint triathlon by sprint triathlon by half-Ironman, until, oops! There it was on my schedule.

So much of life is this: gaining exposure to things until they become normal. It used to be that, over after-work drinks, my friend Alan would ask about whatever adventure race I was competing in that weekend, and then shake his head: "That's crazy. You're on the racecourse for how long? What do you eat? How do you pee?" But then, one day, as I lamented all the things I had stacked up for the weekend, he said, "What length race is it?"

"Sprint," I said mournfully, eagerly awaiting the onrush of sympathy I'd become accustomed to receiving from Alan.

"Oh," he said, reaching for his drink and nodding decisively, "No big deal. Half-day. You'll be done in time for dinner."

Aside from the slightly sinking sensation that I'd have to find something else to do to impress Alan, I was also weirdly tickled that he had become one of us, even having never participated in the sport.

*   *   *   *

When I go for runs or rides, walks or hikes, I sometimes post them to an app called Strava. It tells people what I've done for training that day, and people can give me thumbs up or make comments on my profile. And my smartwatch connects me to people who are training for similar events, if I want.

But more frequently, what happens as I'm outside running on or my bicycle is that I write tweets or Facebook posts in my head, collecting experiences, sights, smells to relay to people:

Fog makes eucalyptus, pepper smell super prominent today, I might tweet.

Or, "One two three four five six seven bunnies today! Plus two fat mourning doves and a coffee klatch of crows."

Or, "One BBQ, one mattress, one green bin full of gigantic palm fronds out for collection today. Wonder who will take the BBQ and mattress?"

If these tweets aren't exactly popular, I like to think that they're doing something else, for both me and my readers: They are, I think, sending out sending out this message:

"Hello! I am here, doing these things. Sometimes I feel lonely, and I wonder if there are any of you out there. I think you are out there.

"If any of you ever wondered if you could or should do these things I am doing, the answer is yes. You can. Come join me.

"You are welcome here. You belong."

I think we all need to hear this every once in awhile, to remind ourselves that our space is wherever it is we want. And also, that if we want to go there, we probably are not going alone. Someone has gone before us. Someone will go after us.

There are lots of ways to be a token. An inspiration. A pioneer, an explorer, a woman in this world. When I read about or see Black women hiking the Appalachian Trail alone, or when I talk to my Latina friend about the three weeks she spent alone in Gettysburg for a writer's residency, I feel a deep sense of gratitude. But I am also keenly aware that they are not doing it for me. They have done this thing for themselves. They have made the decision I am not able to come to yet: That this mountain vista, or that clear lake, this experience of having done this thing you have always wanted to do, is worth potential bodily harm. It is worth having to walk past a landscape peppered with Confederate flags. It is worth having to smile weakly at that old hoary nut: "Well! Don't see many of you around!"

What these women carry around with them is conviction.

This I lack, in spades, when it comes to my place in the outdoors life.

I have a long way to go, yet. And I also know that if I still lived in Taiwan, or anywhere in Asia, I wouldn't have this problem. I would just be another Asian woman, out on the trails of Asia, enjoying herself. (For a woman, spending days out in the woods alone is still weird in Asia. But at least I wouldn't be at risk of bodily harm just because of my ethnicity.)

For now, though, I think I must just keep plugging away at my own Appalachian trail of an ambition: I must continue to seek to make normal the things I want to keep on doing long into my old age.

The posts I write about my activities in the outdoors can, I hope, be articles on someone's wall. Maybe these posts are in the vein of the women who came before me: Existing quietly in the background, waiting for someone to see them. That would be okay.

And then, even if no one does see them, It would still be my job, to determinedly get on with the task of doing whatever I want to do. This is perhaps my biggest aspiration, my runner's high, my most consistent version of summiting peaks: that moment when you're flying, alone on the path or the road or the trail, on foot or on bike, and you've forgotten that you are different. For a couple of seconds, with the sky wide open above you and the road stretching ahead, the payoff for daring is normalcy.

ACKNOWLEDGEMENTS

The women who taught me it was okay to be a newbie: Jody, Betsy, Jen.

The men who taught me how to, uh, sport: Rob, Scott, Andy, Marc, Chris, Steve, Peter, Robert, Jim.

Edna Brush Perkins, who came before me and whose story I will always tell.

The people who listened to me yammer on and on about this topic, and then voluntarily read its first draft: Mike Smith, John Brantingham, Andy Seiple, Kelly Davio, Désirée Zamorano, Tom Greenman, Kate Siber, Jim Gearhart, Iris Graville, Heather Durham.

Leslie M. Browning, who makes a writer feel heard.

Rosalie Morales Kearns, my first publisher and forever cheerleader.

The women in Lisa's critique group, whose very existences inspire me to write on, and who read and critiqued part of this work: Xochitl, Beverly, Lisa herself, Lauren, Rachael.

My bicycles, Grub and Poutine.

My dead dog, Sprocket, whose presence helped me to claim more space in this outdoor world.

The women who race on, and whose accomplishments provide me with ever higher aspirations: You go, girls.

REFERENCES

Data about Carmel-by-the-Sea, CA was accessed from data.io on November 13, 2019.

The quote about Anna Bissell's sales style is from the Eagle Leadership Center's web site: https://www.eaglecenterforleadership.com/single-post/2016/05/25/Leaders-in-History-Anna-Bissell (Accessed November 13, 2019.)

Rahawa Haile's wonderful article on her experience on the Appalachian Trail, "Going It Alone," can be found in *Outside* Magazine's online edition, April 11, 2017.

The quote about Edna Brush Perkins is from Case Western University's web site. https://case.edu/ech/articles/p/perkins-edna-brush (Accessed November 13, 2019.)

The *London Spectator*'s review of Edna Brush Perkins' *The White Heart of the Mojave* is real humdinger. It was published on April 21, 1923, and you can read it in their digital archives.

ABOUT THE AUTHOR

Yi Shun Lai (say "yeeshun" for her first name; "lie" for her last) is the fiction editor and co-publisher of the *Tahoma Literary Review*. She has dabbled in a great many sports ranging from rock climbing to orienteering and mountain biking and is proficient at most of them.

She teaches in the MFA programs at Bay Path University and Southern New Hampshire University. Her column on writing and publishing, "From the Front Lines," appears every month in *The Writer* magazine. Her debut novel, *Not a Self-Help Book: The Misadventures of Marty Wu,* is in its fourth printing. Web: thegooddirt.org; Twitter @gooddirt

LITTLE
BOUND BOOKS

THE LITTLE BOUND BOOKS ESSAY SERIES